How High I Fly

by Tom Riedel

Published by Is It Wet Yet, Press ©2023

Acknowledgments

The story's inspiration stemmed from vivid dreams of flying. This overwhelming feeling inspired me to put pen to paper, leading to the birth of this story. I hope the book sparks wonder and exploration in readers, motivating them to record their own dreams.

I would like to extend my heartfelt thanks to my friends Kevin and Jim for their unwavering support and invaluable contributions to this book. Their keen eye and thoughtful critiques have helped shape this work into what it is today. I am deeply grateful for their encouragement along the way. Thank you, Kevin and Jim, for being there every step of the way. Your friendship means the world to me.

My gratitude also goes out to the assistance I received from ChatGPT during the creation of this book.

Chapters

Chapter One

Eva's First Float

▲ ▲ ▲

AFTER SCHOOL, ON A TYPICAL afternoon. Eva and her best friend Jas were walking home together.

Jas was the eldest of six children, raised in a bustling household that was always filled with laughter and noise. She was a natural leader, taking charge of her younger siblings whenever her parents were busy. She was driven and always pushed herself to be the best in her class, hoping to make her parents proud.

Eva, on the other hand, was an only child and often felt lonely growing up. Her parents were both successful business people who were always busy and never had much time for her. Despite their love and support, Eva struggled in school, constantly comparing herself to her classmates and feeling inadequate.

The girls had met in middle school and quickly became friends. They bonded over their differences and found comfort in each other's company. Jas was drawn to Eva's carefree spirit, while Eva was envious of Jas's confidence and drive. They each longed for the life of the other and found a sense of balance in their friendship.

Walking along the sidewalk, the two girls chatted about their day and all the exciting things that had happened at school. Suddenly, Eva's thoughts drifted to the upcoming school dance. She had a secret crush on a boy in her class, and she couldn't stop thinking about the possibility of him asking her to the dance. She visualized herself twirling in her beloved attire.

As Eva daydreamed about the dance, she suddenly felt a strange flutter in her stomach. She instinctively closed her eyes as she continued to stroll forward next to Jas. Her eyelids shut of their own own as she walked along behind Jas. With each new stride, the sensation of weightlessness increased, until it seemed as if her feet were floating on air. To her utter shock, she opened her eyes and realized she was suspended in midair.

"Jas, look at me!" Eva let out a squeal of delight.

Jas's eyes widened in disbelief. "How... How are you doing that?"

Eva was at a loss for words. All she knew was that she was lost in fantasy over the dance one minute, and then floating on air the next. This seemingly supernatural reaction seemed to have been sparked by her feeling of elation. She felt like a balloon, floating uncontrollably towards the treetops.

"What's happening to me? Am I dreaming?", Eva blurted as mixed feelings of confusion and wonder flooded her mind.

Jas, regaining her composure, replied, "No, you're definitely not dreaming. You're actually floating!" Eva was both excited and scared by her new found ability. She had never felt anything like it before.

As she drifted higher and higher, Eva's curiosity took over. She tried to control her flight, concentrating her thoughts. But the more she tried to control it, the less ability she had. She found herself sinking back to the ground.

"What's happening? I lost it." Eva stammered.

Jas thought for a moment. "Maybe it's like trying to force a puzzle piece to fit. It's not going to work until you relax and allow it to fall into place."

Eva took a deep breath and closed her eyes. She let her mind calm down and let go of her need to control the situation. And just like that, she was floating again.

"You're right, Jas. It's not about thinking, it's about feeling," Eva said with a smile. "...but how will I avoid birds and power lines?" She touched down gently once again.

Jas and Eva were both in shock and couldn't believe what they had just seen.

They decided to go home for now and try her powers another day. To keep this secret, they would have to devise a strategy. Eva was gripped by the fear that someone would find out about her powers and that the adults would cage her like a pet bird.

They walked home in silence, each lost in their own thoughts. Eva couldn't wait to explore her new abilities further, but she also knew that she had to tread carefully. The significance of this event almost caused her to forget about the dance... *Almost*.

Astonished, Jas remarked, "I can't believe it," as they walked through the park. "You're like a superhero or something!"

"I know, right?" Eva replied. Excitement brimmed in her voice. "It's like my body just knew what to do. I didn't even have to think about it."

"We should totally fly around the city and fight crime!" Jas said, as her eyes glistened in delight.

Eva remarked with doubt in her voice, "I don't know about that. I'm still not sure how to control it. This happened by accident when I was not paying attention at all, but as soon as I thought about controlling it, I fell back down."

Jas gave a deadpan nod, "Right. I mean, it's like your mood swings have superpowers or something."

"Exactly!" Eva commented. "But what if I can't control it? What if I float away and can't come back down? Or what if someone sees me?"

"Don't worry," Jas said, putting a comforting arm around her friend's shoulders. "We'll figure it out together. And if anyone does see us, we'll just say we're practicing for the next 'Superheroes Got Talent' competition."

The girls laughed and continued to walk, their minds racing with possibilities. As they reached the corner of their street, Eva turned to Jas.

"I think we should meet up and practice sometime. See if we can figure out how to navigate."

Jas responded with an enthusiastic nod. "Yeah, let's do it! We'll be like a dynamic duo."

The two friends glanced at each other and laughed, then rushed off in different directions towards their respective homes, eager to explore this new ability and see just how high they could fly.

On a phone call later that night, the duo made plans to continue their exploration of Eva's new powers. They both knew it would take time and patience to fully harness her potential, but the thrill of discovery and the unknown had them hooked.

▲ ▲ ▲

Chapter Two

Navigating the Skies

▲ ▲ ▲

WHILE STROLLING THROUGH THE PARK, Eva and Jas stopped to watch the clouds float by. Without warning, Eva began to levitate uncontrollably into the air. Luckily, no one was around to witness the incident. Jas knew she had to act fast before anyone saw. "Eva!" Jas shouted, leaping as high as she could to grab Eva's foot. Eva struggled to speak, but managed to let out a faint "What the?"

As she swung from Eva's shoe, Jas could feel the extra weight gradually bringing them back down to earth. The shoe began to slip off Eva's foot, and for a moment, it seemed like they were both in for a very bad day. But Jas summoned every ounce of courage she had. She readjusted her grip with both hands and interlaced her fingers into Eva's shoe laces, which helped constrict the shoe tightly around Eva's foot.

Jas could feel the extra weight gradually bringing them back down to earth. As Jas swung from Eva's shoe, her heart was pounding with a mix of fear and exhilaration. She knew the gravity of the situation and the potential danger if she couldn't bring them back to earth safely. They eventually landed back on solid ground, Jas anchoring Eva until she was on firm footing.

"That was a close one!" exclaimed Jas through rapid breaths, her heart still pumping with adrenaline. "Thank goodness you were there to catch me!" Eva said, hugging Jas tightly.

Eva looked at Jas with a mixture of gratitude and embarrassment. "I don't know what happened, I just suddenly couldn't control it."

Jas reassured her best friend, "It's okay, we'll figure it out."

A few more days went by. They had been trying to figure out how to control Eva's powers, but it seemed like a never-ending struggle.

"I just can't seem to get the hang of it," Eva said in frustration.

"Don't worry, we'll figure it out," Jas reassured her. "It's all about quieting your thoughts down."

"But how do I do that?" Eva asked, with just a whiff of despair in her voice.

"Well, it's like trying to fly a kite," Jas said, with a twinkle in her eye. "You have to let the kite fly, but you also need a firm grasp on the string. Don't focus too much on the string, or you miss out on the flight. Keep your attention on the kite."

Eva nodded, determined to improve. They spent the next few weeks practicing in a secluded field, far from prying eyes. Eva found that by focusing on her breathing and visualizing herself staying grounded, she was able to keep her powers in check.

As they practiced, Eva's confidence grew. One day, she noticed that when she took off her shoes and was barefoot, she felt more free. At first, she thought it was just a superstition, like some athletes who believe that they perform better with a lucky rabbit's foot. But as she continued to practice with her bare feet, she realized that it truly made a difference in her ability to manage her powers. She felt more in tune with the elements around her, allowing her to focus better on her breathing and visualization techniques. From that point on, whenever she trained, she made sure to kick off her shoes and feel the earth beneath her feet.

On a clear day, Eva was getting the hang of flying. Just as she touched down for a successful landing, the girls were interrupted by a familiar voice.

"What are you girls up to out here?" said Noah Pumwinkle, the school's sensitivity counselor, as he approached them with a self-important swagger. But just as he was about to ask his usual barrage of nosy questions, he tripped over Eva's shoes and stumbled, causing his coffee to spill all over his shirt. The hot liquid soaked through his shirt and onto his skin, causing him to yelp in pain.

Eva and Jas stifled their laughter as Noah frantically tried to wipe off the coffee. "Oh, don't mind me," he said through gritted teeth, trying to play it off cool. "I just came to check in on you two." Noah had a reputation for finding ways to insert himself into the students' personal lives and offer his unsolicited advice.

Noah had taken to calling himself by his first name in an attempt to seem more approachable, but students saw right through the facade and nicknamed him "Nosey Noah" behind his back. Despite his misguided attempts to connect with the students, the girls couldn't help but roll their eyes at his pretentious behavior.

"What do you kids think you're doing out here?" Noah asked, dripping with fake concern. "You're not feeling isolated, are you?"

Jas, always quick with a witty retort, replied, "Oh, just catching some rays and getting some exercise, Noah. You know, the healthy stuff."

"I see," Noah said, his eyes scanning the field suspiciously. "Just remember, I'm here for all of you. If anyone is feeling affected by micro-aggressions, my office is always open as a safe space for you to talk about it. Let's not forget, staying silent is just as harmful as the aggressions themselves."

Eva and Jas exchanged a knowing look, both growing weary of his long-winded lectures. They had heard it all before.

"Sure thing." Jas said, trying to sound as innocent as possible. "We'll keep that in mind."

Nosey Noah gave them one last skeptical look, his eyes scanning their faces as if trying to read their thoughts. Eva and Jas both tried to keep their expressions neutral, not wanting to give him anything to use against them. They knew that he didn't trust them and that he suspected that they were up to something. The tension in the air was palpable. Noah made his way back inside. As soon as he was out of sight, Eva and Jas let out a sigh of relief.

"That was close," Eva said.

"Yeah, I thought he was going to figure us out for sure," Jas said.

"We have to be more careful," Eva said. "We can't let anyone else find out about my powers."

"Agreed," Jas said. "But for now, let's call it a day. We can come back and practice more tomorrow when it's safer."

And with that, the two of them headed home, the thrill of their secret powers and the need for caution weighing heavily on their minds.

▲ ▲ ▲

Chapter Three

Flight Buddies

▲ ▲ ▲

I T WAS A CLEAR, SUNNY weekend day when Eva and Jas decided to meet at the field behind their school to meet when nobody was around. During a low fly-by, Eva playfully reached out to give Jas a high-five. To her surprise, when their hands made contact, Jas suddenly lifted off the ground and floated along for a few brief moments before softly landing on her feet.

"Whoa!" Jas exclaimed. "What just happened?!"

"I don't know!" Eva shouted back, excitement and confusion evident in her voice. "But let's try it again!"

Jas's face lit up. "Let's do it! Let's fly now!"

They walked to the edge of the park and found a secluded spot behind a large tree. Eva took a deep breath and closed her eyes, trying to clear her mind. She tried to let go of everything that was bothering her. Her body loosened up and she started to breathe more easily. A familiar sensation of lightening came over Eva and soon she was floating only a foot or so above the ground. It was a peculiar yet thrilling experience. She opened her eyes and looked around, taking in the view from her new vantage point.

The leaves of the tree rustled in the breeze, and Eva could see the tops of buildings in the distance. She felt a sense of freedom and lightness, as if she could fly away at any moment. She closed her eyes again and let herself drift, enjoying the sensation of weightlessness.

Jas called up to Eva, "Hey, did you forget about me?".

Eva was prepared and able to come back down to the ground. Still hovering a few feet above Jas, she rotated her body into a horizontal position. Facing downwards, she extended one arm within reach of Jas.

"Take my hand," she called down to Jas. The tranquility in Eva's voice instilled a sense of ease in Jas.

Jas eagerly reached up and grabbed Eva's hand. As soon as they made contact, Jas felt a surge of energy. It was as if a switch had been flipped, and suddenly she was weightless, her feet lifting off the ground with ease. The sensation was exhilarating, and she couldn't help but let out a laugh of pure joy.

"Alright, let's do this! I'm ready to boldly go..." she said, channeling her inner Star Trek character.

Eva chuckled. "Well, we might not be in space, but I'm definitely ready to explore some new territories," she replied, joining in on the fun.

"Ready for warp speed?" Eva replied, a big grin spreading across her face.

Jas grinned and squeezed Eva's hand, "Indeed, Captain Janeway!"

A sense of freedom and lightness came over Jas. She had never experienced this before. It was as if she were truly flying. As the world below became smaller, the sky was the limit. They enjoyed the warm sun on their skin and the wind rushing through their hair.

Eva and Jas soared through the sky, their arms outstretched as they pretended to fly the USS Voyager.

"Captain Janeway to Tuvok, do you read me?" Eva called out in her best Katherine Hepburn impression.

"Reading you loud and clear, Captain," Jas replied, channeling her inner Tuvok.

As they flew, they pointed out different objects and animals below them, imagining they were discovering new and exotic alien worlds.

"Captain, I'm picking up strange readings from that group of cows down there," Jas said in her most serious Tuvok tone.

"Tuvok, I think we should beam down and investigate," Eva said, playing along.

They swooped down, pretending to beam onto the field below and "investigate" the cows. As they ventured into uncharted territory, Eva decided to take a closer look by touching down. Unfortunately, Jas's left foot made a less-than-graceful landing directly into a steaming pile of cow poo.

Eva, who was flying nearby, noticed her friend's predicament and burst into laughter. "Ahh, it's got you!" she exclaimed, pretending to be attacked by an alien slime creature. "Quick, I'll save you!"

Jas tried to maintain her composure, but the smell and goo from the cow poop were making it hard for her to keep a straight face. "Help! Get it off! Get it off!" she cried, shaking her leg.

Eva flew over and hovered above her friend, pointing at the cow poop and making silly alien noises. "I'll blast it with my phaser, hold on!" she said in a dramatic voice, pretending to be Janeway.

As the girls wiped the mess from Jas's shoe, they heard the sound of a farmer shuffling around in his nearby shed. Eva's eyes grew wide.

"Klingons!" Jas whispered, as she tried to suppress her emotions with the stoicism of Commander Tuvok.

"Quick, Tuvok, set a course for the nearest Starfleet base!" Eva ordered urgently, her eyes darting back and forth between the farmer and the leftover signs of the supposed "alien slime."

Jas nodded, trying to stifle a giggle. She reached for Eva's hand, their fingers intertwining in a tight grip.

Just as the farmer emerged from the shed, the girls cleared the rooftop, out of sight. They could hear the farmer muttering as he scratched his head, completely bewildered by the mysterious presence.

Eva and Jas didn't stop to look back. They were too busy laughing and whooping with joy, their cheeks flushed with the thrill of their narrow escape.

"That was close, Captain," Jas said, mimicking Tuvok's characteristic raised eyebrow. "I think we need to be more careful with our landings in the future."

"Agreed, Tuvok," Eva replied with a grin. "We'll make sure to stay clear of Klingon territory in the future."

As they flew back up, they couldn't help but burst out laughing at the absurdity of it all.

"Captain, I must report that the cows are friendly," Jas said, trying to stifle her laughter.

"Excellent work, Tuvok," Eva replied, giggling.

They continued their pretend mission, acting out their favorite scenes from Star Trek, laughing and having a great time as they explored the world from a new perspective.

They flew over the treetops, feeling a rush of excitement as they swooped down and then rose back up again. The wind in their hair and the freedom of flight made them feel alive. They zoomed faster and higher, their laughter echoing through the trees below. They performed acrobatic flips and turns in the air, enjoying the sensation of weightlessness.

It was as if they were birds, free to go wherever they wanted. The exhilaration of the flight filled them with joy, and for that moment, nothing else mattered. They were completely in the moment, living in the freedom of their flight.

They flew over the treetops and swooped down to the ground, feeling the wind in their hair and the freedom of flight. They soared through the sky, experiencing the sensation of weightlessness and the thrill of flying at high speeds.

The two girls spent the next few hours testing different ways to initiate and maintain their tandem flight. They learned that they had to stay in direct contact to fly together and that it was easier to stay in the air when they were in tandem.

When in solo flight, Eva often noticed thoughts of worry creeping into her mind, which disrupted her ability to stay in the air. But when flying together, her attention was solely on the task at hand. Their movements became more synchronized and effortless.

As they soared through the sky, hand in hand, Eva felt a sense of calm wash over her. The worry that often plagued her during solo flights was nowhere to be found. Instead, her focus was solely on the present moment and the thrill of flying with her best friend.

"This is amazing, Jas!" Eva shouted over the wind. "I feel like I can do anything when I'm up here with you!"

Jas grinned back, her eyes sparkling with excitement. "Me too! Flying together just makes everything easier. We're unstoppable!"

They continued to soar through the air, their movements becoming more and more in sync with each other. They laughed and shouted, their joy contagious, and their adventure together truly unforgettable.

"This is the life, Captain!" Jas said, pretending to be her favorite Star Trek character.

"Indeed, Tuvok," Eva replied, taking on her own Star Trek persona.

Carefree and without a worry, the duo ventured out over a tranquil lake. Then, in an instant, a gust of wind caught Jas off guard. The turbulence put her into a spiral, and she lost her grip on Eva's hand. Jas panicked as she felt herself falling, her screams echoing across the lake. She could see the water getting closer and closer. Time seemed to halt as Jas feared she would plummet into the lake and be lost forever.

"Jas!" Eva shouted, diving after her.

Eva's heart raced as she watched Jas fall. She willed herself downward with increasing speed, her arms reaching out towards Jas. Her eyes were locked on Jas' outstretched hands. It felt like an eternity as she closed the distance between them. With a final burst of speed, Eva caught up with Jas and wrapped both arms around her securely.

The two girls' arms locked together around each other's bodies as they felt the jolt of contact.

Jas clung to Eva, her body shaking with adrenaline. "Thank you," she gasped. "Thank you for saving me." They landed safely on a nearby rooftop, both of them panting and shaken.

"That was too close," Jas said, her voice trembling.

"I'm sorry," Eva said, her eyes filling with tears. "I should have been more careful."

"No, it's not your fault," Jas said, putting a steady hand on her shoulder. "We just need to be more careful from now on. It wouldn't hurt to read the weather reports, either."

From that day on, they were more cautious when flying together. They learned to do what every good pilot does by checking the day's wind speeds and weather conditions before going out. They studied wind patterns, and made sure to fly during times when the winds were calm, or at least manageable. They also made sure to fly closer to the ground, so that if anything went wrong, they would have a better chance of recovering.

They also established their own set of protocols, just like their favorite Starfleet officers. They were prepared for any unexpected encounters with rogue planets or hostile aliens, determined to always stay one step ahead of danger.

"Engage!" Eva shouted.

▲ ▲ ▲

Chapter Four

Nosey Noah

▲ ▲ ▲

W ITH EVA STEADILY IMPROVING HER command of her powers, she and Jas found themselves up against a new hurdle. People in their town started to notice that strange things were happening and they suspected that someone with unusual abilities might be behind it. They started speculating that it could be a vigilante, a ghost or even an alien.

The girls knew that fresh tactics were required to keep their secret safe. They thought about ways to use their powers in a way that wouldn't draw attention to themselves.

As Eva continued to learn to control her powers, she and Jas also had to endure the seemingly continuous scrutiny of Nosey Noah. He became suspicious and paid close attention to their activities and would frequently ask them questions, trying to figure out what they were up to. Occasionally he said things that made them feel like he definitely knew their secret.

"How about the weather we're having today?" Noah would casually quip, as the girls walked past his open office door. Other times he would mention how lovely the sky was. These remarks cut close to the bone and both girls were feeling like bugs under a microscope.

The heavy burden of keeping their secret from Nosey Noah was taking a toll on Eva. Her powers were becoming weaker and weaker. Jas noticed that the more anxious they became, the harder it was for Eva to manifest her flying ability. They were at a loss, unsure of what to do. One day, during a particularly anxious moment, Eva's powers failed her completely and she got stuck in a tree.

The pressure was on for Eva and Jas, they knew they had to do something. They were worried that if Nosey Noah found out about their powers, he could expose their secret. Who knows where that would lead.

Eva imagined being dissected in some dark, secluded government laboratory or being locked away in a cell deep inside Area 51 with real aliens and bigfoot as her only companions.

Jas and Eva would relieve their tensions by playfully predicting the wildest scenarios that would happen if they were caught. Taking their fears to absurd levels together made them realize how silly they were being. Still, the girls had no certainty whether their fears were justified or not.

"What if they kept us in a glass box," Jas wondered aloud, "like animals in a zoo." Both girls lamented the idea of watching the sky through a window, forever longing to be set free.

Meanwhile, the duo tried to avoid Nosey Noah as much as possible, but it was difficult to shake him off. The constant anxiety and pressure muted Eva's abilities. She couldn't fly anymore, and that made her and Jas even more worried. She began to feel trapped.

Jas realized they had to act fast if they wanted to regain Eva's powers. The girls knew they needed to come up with a plan to take the focus off of them and distract Noah from his investigation.

On a fateful day while walking past the abandoned movie theater, the girls stumbled upon a flyer that caught their attention. It depicted the dire situation of a tiny South American country where access to clean water was scarce.

The headline, written in bold letters, read, "Digging wells, planting hope." Jas couldn't help but quip, "Dig a well, fill a nosy counselor's time." The girls shared an ornery chuckle. They knew they had found their solution.

The dubious counselor, always eager to showcase his virtue, would not be able to resist the opportunity to spend the next few months in a remote and sweaty village, doing hard labor to prove his virtue.

The very next day, with a certain amount of apprehension, Jas entered Noah's office and presented the idea to him. She explained that the people in the country were in dire need of clean water and that only he could make a real difference. Jas emphasized that it would be a great opportunity for him to make a difference and to gain a new perspective on life, living as he does in relative comfort.

"I don't know..." Noah hesitated as Jas and Eva explained the opportunity to him. "It sounds risky."

"Come on, Noah," Jas implored. "You're always talking about wanting to make a difference in the world. This is your chance to do something real."

"Think of the people in the country," Eva added. "They're counting on us. You can't let them down."

Noah rubbed the back of his neck, feeling torn. He wanted to help, but he also had obligations at the school. But finally Jas's concern for the people in the country touched him, and he realized that this was an opportunity he couldn't pass up.

"Okay," he said with a nod. "I'll do it. I'll make travel arrangements and start preparing for the trip."

As Noah became more and more preoccupied with his new mission, the girls were able to relax. Eva's powers slowly came back to her, and she was able to fly again. The duo no longer felt like they were being watched, and they were finally able to breathe easy again. With Noah's attention elsewhere, they were able to proceed without distraction.

Although the girls knew that Nosey Noah would eventually return, they were grateful for the time they had had to regroup. For Eva, this meant that her powers would surely come back to her. She had been struggling with her ability to fly for some time. Under Noah's constant scrutiny, she had been unable to tap into her abilities. But now, with the pressure lifted, she would finally be able to let her powers flow.

Jas was happy for her friend and eager for their adventure to resume. Her natural talent for coming up with creative solutions proved useful once again, as she was able to navigate any social obstacles that came their way. She had a talent for finding a way around any obstacle.

A week later, Jas and Eva felt a sense of relief as they watched Noah pack his bags and depart for the airport.

As Noah tossed his bags into the trunk of the waiting taxi, Jas and Eva stood on the curb, waving goodbye. "Take care of yourself, Noah!" Jas called out, a smile on her face.

"Don't worry about us," Eva added, her own smile a little more reserved. "We'll be fine."

Noah nodded, a look of determination on his face as he climbed into the back seat of the taxi. "I'll be back before you know it," he said, his voice carrying through the open car window.

The taxi pulled away from the curb and Jas and Eva watched it disappear down the street. "Do you think he'll be okay?" Jas asked, her smile fading.

Eva nodded. "Of course he will. Noah's a big boy, he can handle himself." But even as she said the words, Eva couldn't shake the feeling of unease that settled in the pit of her stomach.

Jas sighed and linked her arm through Eva's. "Well, come on. We've got work to do." And with that, the two girls turned and headed back inside, their thoughts already turning to their next plan.

▲ ▲ ▲

Chapter Five

Clipped Wings

▲ ▲ ▲

FINALLY FREE FROM PRYING EYES, Eva became deeply fascinated by her powers. She would often daydream about all the amazing things she could do with them, from flying high above the clouds to getting to school on time after oversleeping. She also started to realize that her powers could be used for more selfish reasons. She thought about how she could use them to get whatever she wanted, whether it was material possessions or social status.

Eva began to question whether giving in to these temptations would be morally wrong or if it would be within her rights to do so. After all, it was she who had the ability. A little voice inside argued, "Maybe I deserve more."

It started with small things, like fantasizing about winning races at school or impressing her classmates with her incredible agility. But as time went on, Eva's thoughts turned darker. She began to imagine using her powers to get whatever she wanted, whether it was money, fame, or even revenge.

She would daydream about exacting her revenge on those who had wronged her, whether it was a cruel teacher, a mean-spirited classmate, or even a family member who had caused her pain. The more she indulged in this type of thinking, the more it consumed her. She reveled in the idea of making them pay, of showing them that she was not to be underestimated. She would imagine using her powers to humiliate them in front of others, to make them feel small and powerless. The idea of making them suffer felt oddly satisfying, of making them regret the day they ever crossed her.

One of Eva's darker fantasies was about getting revenge on an older boy who had bullied her in the past. She imagined using her powers to fly up to his bedroom window in the middle of the night and scare him with her sudden appearance. In her fantasy, she would then use her powers to lift him out of his bed and hold him suspended in the air.

"Do you remember me?" she chimed, as the bully openly wet his pajamas. She delighted in the thought of him finally being knocked down to size.

She would then fly away into the night sky, leaving him shaken and terrified. This fantasy provided her with a sense of power and control that she didn't have in real life, but it also made her feel guilty for having such thoughts. She reasoned that it would be a matter of justice.

Despite her growing obsession with her powers, Eva managed to keep her thoughts a secret from Jas. Her best friend would never approve of her using her abilities for such purposes, and it could even jeopardize the trust they had built. But the more time Eva spent lost in her imagination, the harder it was for her to resist the pull.

Jas noticed that Eva seemed distant and asked her, "Is everything okay? ...you've been acting strange lately."

"Big test is coming up," replied Eva. It was the first time she had lied to Jas. The situation left her with an uneasy feeling, and she excused herself from the room.

One day, as Eva was preparing for a race at school, she found herself unable to resist the temptation to use her powers to give herself an unfair advantage. As the starting pistol fired, she began to run, keeping her feet just an inch above the ground. At first, her trick was imperceptible, and she was sure she would come in first place—something she had never achieved before. But as she pushed herself harder and faster, she suddenly fell flat on her face in front of everyone.

Confused and embarrassed, Eva quickly got up and tried to make her way to the finish line. But as she trudged along the ground, she realized that her powers were completely gone. She had abused them, and now they had deserted her.

Feeling ashamed and with nowhere else to turn, Eva approached

Jas to tell her what had happened. Jas listened patiently but didn't seem surprised by the news. "I told you this would happen," she said. "Your powers have a self-regulating feedback loop that prevents them from being abused."

Eva felt a knot form in her stomach as she realized the full extent of her mistake. She had let her ego get in the way, and now she had lost her powers.

Jas continued, "I'm willing to help you, but you need to understand that this is serious." "This is not something you can just brush off and forget about."

Eva nodded with tears streaming down her cheeks. She knew that she had a lot of work ahead of her if she wanted to regain Jas' trust and her powers.

Eva hung her head, knowing that Jas was right. She had let her selfish desires cloud her judgment, and now she was paying the price. The thought occurred to her that perhaps her ability was not a gift but a curse. Conquering temptation would be an added challenge for her to contend with. From that day on, she made a conscious effort to control herself, not indulge in pointless fantasy, and never again let her ego get the best of her. She knew that she had no choice, since her powers would disappear if misused.

Jas placed a hand on Eva's shoulder, sensing her distress. "It's not easy, but it's worth it," she said, with a smile. "Don't forget, I'm here for you."

With a nod, Eva knew that she was not alone in her struggles, and with Jas's guidance, she could overcome this setback. The two girls hugged each other, making a silent promise of mutual support. From that moment on, they would work to make sure Eva would not fall into the same trap again. The journey would be challenging, but together they would navigate it.

As Eva sat on the couch, scrolling through her phone, she suddenly felt the urge to use her powers for a silly prank. She glanced over at Jas, who was sound asleep, and the mischievous thought grew stronger. But just as she was about to levitate herself directly above Jas and yell "Boo" to shock her, she remembered their recent lessons on self-discipline. She let out a sigh, smiled at the thought of her own silly idea, and put her phone down, determined to resist the urge.

Just then, Jas stirred and rubbed her eyes, "What's up?" she asked, noticing Eva's expression.

"Oh, just fighting the urge to prank you." Eva said with a grin.

"Ha! Well, you're doing a great job," Jas said, sitting up. "But who knows how long you'll be able to resist. I'll have to sleep with one eye open from now on."

▲ ▲ ▲

Chapter Six

How Could You?

▲ ▲ ▲

J AS WAS ALWAYS THERE FOR Eva, the girl with the gift of flight. She had never been envious of Eva's powers and had always been there to cheer her on, even as Eva struggled to come to terms with the weight of her newfound abilities. As the school year progressed, though, Jas began to feel the weight of keeping such a huge secret to herself.

On a sunny afternoon, Jas walked home from school, lost in her thoughts. "Everyone around me seems to have exciting lives, and here

I am, holding onto something that could blow their minds." she wondered silently. "I know it's not just me carrying this burden, but still, I feel like I'm going to burst."

She recalled her family members constantly asking her why she had been so quiet lately. "They have no idea what I'm bearing" she thought. "But who could I trust with something this big?"

She sighed and continued her walk, the weight of the secret seeming heavier than ever before.

Jas's cousin, Jake was always up to something new and exciting. Growing up, he was the cool cousin who had all the stories and was the life of the party. Nevertheless, under pressure, Jas chose to confide in Jake about Eva's powers.

"Promise me you won't tell a soul!" Jas implored him before she agreed to share the news of Eva's powers. "No problem." Jake replied with a look of awe in his eyes.

But Jake's self-control was even weaker, and after he heard about Eva's powers, he couldn't resist gossiping with his friends, and soon, word of Eva's powers began to spread like wildfire. Jas was devastated, knowing that her decision had led to this.

It wasn't long before the gossip spread throughout the school, and people were divided on whether to believe it or not. Some were convinced that it was all just a rumor, while others were convinced that it was true. Eva, who had always been private about her powers, found herself the center of attention. She was constantly bombarded with questions and requests to demonstrate her abilities. It was a difficult time for her and she struggled to adapt to the sudden influx of attention.

Some of the students thought Jas was just making it up and that she was a pathological liar looking for attention. Others thought she was delusional and needed to see a therapist. Some on the extreme fringes even believed she was a bird trapped in a girl's body and should demand a change of gender. But a growing number of students actually believed her, and they started to investigate. Some would just mock her with taunts such as, "Fly Eva, fly!"

Eva was devastated. "Jas, how could you do this to me?" "I trusted you!" She exclaimed with tears in her eyes.

"I'm sorry, Eva. I didn't mean to hurt you. "My cousin promised me he wouldn't tell anyone," Jas replied with deep remorse.

The situation became so intense that Jas and Eva had to avoid each other at school. They might meet up after classes, but they couldn't be seen together in public. They both felt betrayed, but Jas couldn't help feeling guilty for what she had done. She had broken Eva's trust, and now their friendship was suffering as a result.

Jas knew that her actions had caused Eva a lot of pain, and she wished she could take it all back. Jas struggled with guilt and remorse over her hasty mistake of telling Jake about Eva's powers. She couldn't stop thinking about how Eva's secret was now out in the open and how people were talking about it behind her back. She felt responsible for the way Eva was being treated and wished she had never said anything to Jake.

She tried to apologize to Eva multiple times, but Eva was too hurt and refused to speak to her. Jas felt helpless and didn't know what to do to make things right. Jas tried calling, texting, sending smoke signals, and even tried to bribe the birds to deliver a message to Eva, but nothing seemed to work. She felt like she had lost her BFF and it was all because of her big mouth.

Jas tried to lighten the mood by cracking a joke to herself. "Well, I guess I'll just have to live out the rest of my days as the unluckiest secret keeper in the world," she thought. But deep down, she knew it was no laughing matter.

As Eva struggled with the betrayal of trust from her best friend, she began to question whether or not she could forgive. She felt a deep sense of hurt and betrayal, as if a part of her had been exposed without her consent. Her once-private world had been laid bare for all to see and judge. The thought of facing her classmates and their reactions made her feel incredibly vulnerable and exposed. She felt like she was living in a fishbowl, and all eyes were on her. She couldn't shake the feeling that everyone was talking about her behind her back.

She questioned whether or not their friendship was salvageable, and whether or not she would ever be able to trust Jas again. It was a heavy burden that she felt alone and unable to handle. Her heart ached at the prospect of losing their friendship, but she knew, deep down, that Jas had made a mistake. It was a mistake that Eva could also have made, giving in to strong temptations.

Although it was challenging, she knew that she had to find a way to forgive Jas. Her best friend deserved a another chance. She reminded herself that it is possible to make the best out of a bad situation. She also knew that holding onto resentment and anger would only hurt herself in the long run. Without forgiveness, Eva knew she may never fly again.

So, Eva decided to meet Jas and let her know how she felt. The two girls met in a quiet park, sitting on a bench facing the lake.

Eva took a deep breath and began, "Jas, I know you made a mistake by telling Jake about my powers. I can understand why you did it, but it still hurt me. I was so angry and disappointed."

Jas looked down, ashamed. "I know, and I am so sorry, Eva. I never meant to hurt you." Her lower lip quivered a bit as she paused. "I would do anything to make it up to you."

Eva looked at Jas with a soft gaze and said, "I know you didn't. And I forgive you, Jas." A moment passed in awkward silence between the girls, as a single leaf fell from a tree and landed at their feet.

"I can't imagine my life without you as my best friend." Jas let out a sigh of relief and hugged Eva tightly.

"Thank you, Eva. I promise to never betray your trust again." Eva smiled and hugged her. "I know you won't."

That afternoon, they both agreed to work on rebuilding their trust and vowed to be honest with each other in the future.

The lesson that Eva learned through this experience was that forgiveness is not always easy, but it's necessary. Resentment poisons the person who holds onto it, and it's important to have the courage to forgive and move forward.

▲ ▲ ▲

Chapter Seven

Soaring to New Heights

▲ ▲ ▲

A S THEY WENT BACK TO school Eva and Jas longed keep their bond strong. They knew that they couldn't change the past, but they could learn from their mistakes. They decided to focus on the future and make sure that they never let self-indulgences get in the way of their friendship.

As they walked through the school halls, they were greeted with curious glances and whispered conversations. But the girls didn't let it get to them. They knew that they had a higher purpose and that they had to stay focused on it.

However, the peace didn't last for long, as they soon came across a bully who had a reputation for exploiting the vulnerable.

He sneered, "Oh look who it is, the flying freak. Hey there, high flyer!" The bully licked his lips before continuing. "Come on, give us all a taste of your bird-like abilities!" he taunted with a smirk. "Or are you just all talk and no fly?"

The rest of the students, who had previously been indifferent to the girls, stepped forward to surround the bully, surprising both Eva and Jas.

One student spoke up, "Leave her alone, she's not a freak, she's amazing."

Another chimed in, "Yeah, I'd like to see you take a flying leap!"

The bully fumbled for a response, but the students were quick to cut him off. They began to pepper him with witty one-liners, each one more comical than the last, until the bully was red-faced and sputtering with anger. The students continued to roast him until the tension was broken, and everyone was laughing and joking around. The bully, taken aback by the sudden support, stammered before slinking away. Eva and Jas exchanged a relieved and grateful look, grateful for the unexpected support from their classmates.

A few days passed, and life at school returned to a state of relative normalcy. Eva and Jas were walking down the hall towards their next class when they suddenly heard a familiar voice. Their former adversary, Nosey Noah, had returned from his volunteer expedition sooner than expected, sporting a bandaged hand and a sunburn. Jas and Eva felt a pang of guilt as they knew they had played a part in sending him away, and they felt remorseful for it.

When they entered Noah's office, they felt an immediate shift. The motivational cat calendars, rainbow trinkets, and aggressively worded propaganda posters with various activist slogans that had covered the walls were removed. This new minimalist look was a breath of fresh air for the girls. It no longer felt like they were being shouted at in there. They sensed a similar change in Noah.

"Girls, it's good to see you again." Noah said.

"We're glad to see you too, Noah." Eva remarked, with a trace of trepidation in her voice.

"You seem different." Jas added, observing the change in Noah's demeanor. She nudged Eva as her eyes fixed on his feet. This was the first time the girls had ever seen Noah wear shoes, like a regular adult.

"I've been through a lot these past few months," Noah said, a wistful look in his eyes. "Traveling has a way of putting things into perspective."

To their surprise, Noah didn't hold a grudge. The events of his trip had humbled him greatly. While working on the volunteer irrigation project down in South America, Noah took some seemingly innocuous selfies. He didn't think much of it as he posted the photos online, eager for likes and comments. But in his desire for validation, he had unwittingly put himself in harm's way.

Noah's selfies attracted attention, but from the wrong sort of people. His posts caught the attention of a group of criminals. The gang was able to track Noah down and saw him as an easy target.

In a harrowing turn of events, the thugs lured Noah away from the safety of the camp and proceeded to take advantage of him at a local bar. Meanwhile, other members of the gang broke into his rented room and stole all his possessions. Noah recounted the harrowing experience to Jas and Eva.

Despite being left with only the clothes on his back and his ID, he was able to make it back to the airport. The harsh reality of what happened during his trip left him with much to reflect on during his long, solitary flight home. He realized that acting out of vanity can have severe consequences.

He acknowledged that he had been intrusive and that he understood why they had done what they did. He even offered to help them in any way he could, this time speaking with a newfound sense of humility. His demeanor had become stoic, no longer exuding the flamboyant persona he previously displayed to his students. He requested that they address him formally as "Mr. Pumwinkle" from now on, his previously extravagant attitude now replaced with a more serious and composed one.

The girls gratefully took him up on his offer. Over time, Mr. Pumwinkle became an invaluable asset to their cause, helping them navigate the challenges that came with their powers and use them to benefit those in need. He was glad that he was able to help people in need and he was grateful to be part of their team.

With the help of Mr. Pumwinkle, Jas and Eva established a

charitable organization named The Angels of the Sky. They channeled their efforts towards assisting those in need within their town. The organization quickly gained popularity and success, with many locals turning to them for aid. Realizing the impact they could make, the organization's reach began to expand, reaching out to help more and more people in different areas. They found that they didn't need to travel far to make a difference, they could make a difference right where they were.

Eva's flying ability proved to be a valuable asset when it came to delivering crucial aid during natural disasters. With her powers, the girls were able to reach affected areas quickly and efficiently, providing much-needed food and supplies to those in need. They were also able to reach people stranded by floods and other emergencies faster than traditional rescue teams, making them a valuable addition to the disaster response efforts.

The "Angels of the Sky" were well respected. They were proud of the difference they had made in the world and knew that it would be impossible without the discipline they had built along the way. They learned that forgiveness and compassion are powerful forces that can bring about positive change in the most unlikely places.

Their story of strength and perseverance through difficult times inspired many. They proved that even the most challenging obstacles could be overcome with the support of a friend and that no matter what the world might say, it was possible to be yourself and to find happiness. And as they continued to soar through the sky, spreading hope and positivity wherever they went, the girls remained the best of friends, relying on one another for support and always being there for each other through thick and thin. Their friendship was a shining example to others, and their impact on the world would be felt for generations to come.

With a sudden blaring of the alarm, "Brrranng!", Jas and Eva prepared for their next mission, carefully checking and loading their equipment. They knew that every outing was different and that they had to be ready for anything. zipping up their flight suits, and with one final nod of agreement, they took a deep breath and headed towards the window, ready to take on the world together.

"Are you ready, Jas?" Eva asked with a grin.

"I'm ready, Eva. Let's fly!" Jas exclaimed excitedly.

And with that, they took off into the clouds, ready to face the world as the Angels of the Sky.

▲ ▲ ▲

www.ingramcontent.com/pod-product-compliance
Lightning Source LLC
Chambersburg PA
CBHW070031030426
42335CB00017B/2390